SUCCESS AND FINANCIAL FREEDOM

Passive Income- The Secret Ingredient

Gabor Balogh

Contact and ordering information:
www.facebook.com/gaborbaloghbooks

Dedication

This book is dedicated to my two beautiful daughters, Fiama and Gabriela.

My story at the beginning of this book is ultimately their story. They will be able to reflect on it and remember the journey that was taken many years before they were born.

I am blessed to have them in my life!

Contents

Introduction

I always wanted to write a book to share my thoughts and experience with others.

Since my early 20s I had a burning desire to accomplish more in life so I spent over 25 years looking for answers, studying success principles and successful people. I wanted to understand why some people were more successful than others and why some countries were more successful than others.

I researched different business models, had my own business and spent time with highly successful business people. I read over a hundred books on topics such as Business, Finance, Sales, Marketing, Psychology, Meditation, Personal Development and People Skills. I also listened to hundreds of audio recordings and attended countless seminars and workshops to learn as much as I can.

I have an Honours Business Administration diploma and at the time of writing this book I work in a middle management position for a Toronto Law Firm.

I wanted to share the knowledge I gained and my – at times unique - perspective on success and how to achieve it.

Being successful in life means different things to different people. Success is more complex than most people realize. Financial success is only one component of a balanced and successful life.

In the world of finance there are many experts offering advice, often contradicting each-other's ideas which can be very confusing to many people. This doesn't always mean that one expert is right and the other is wrong. People with financial expertise often focus in on one area – where they have the most experience – and overlook or underestimate other areas that are just as important.

This book – in part – is about developing the right mental attitude to become successful. I will also explain what I perceive to be true Financial Freedom.

I'll give you a few examples of "Financial Vehicles" or different methods to reach it with some basic explanation for each area to get you thinking. These are NOT "Get-Rich-Quick" formulas. The problem with that approach is that even if someone acquired wealth very quickly, in most cases they wouldn't have time to develop the mindset and wisdom to handle that level of financial success. They would probably lose it just as quickly.

You could become a millionaire by winning the lottery but you would not be able to stay there long unless you developed a millionaire mindset. Before you can enjoy lasting success you have to develop the person in the mirror, you have to grow as a person.

Disclaimer - How to use this book

I am not a licensed financial professional therefore my intention is not to give you specific financial advice.

You should never take financial advice from a book regardless of who wrote it. There are many different circumstances and everyone's situation is unique. A book can open your mind and make you think bigger, inspire you and give you ideas you haven't thought of, get you to take action...but a book "doesn't know you personally" therefore you still have to consult with someone who understands your goals, circumstances and even the way you think.

You see, every person who reads a book will have a somewhat different interpretation. Our previous experiences and the level of knowledge we have gained up to this point will act as a filter to process information.

Imagine a book written in such a way that 90% of the book is in English, 10% in a different language. An

English speaker would have a reasonably good idea of what the book is about but could still miss some important points. Now, if someone speaks both languages that person will have a very clear understanding of the book's message.

When you're trying to learn from a book, you also have to keep in mind where the author lives. If you, the reader live in a different country, not everything will apply to your circumstances.

My sincere hope is that this book will add value to your life.

My Story

Szekszard, Hungary – picture by Gabor Balogh

Hungary - I grew up in a town called Szekszard in Hungary, located in Eastern Europe.

I've always been very close to my friends and family. I had a great childhood and did not notice that we didn't have that much growing up. We were not poor by any means as I grew up in a nice house my parents built. Hungary is a beautiful country with a lot of history and I am proud of my heritage. However, we were limited financially compared to Western European or North American countries. This seemed normal in my younger years but as I grew older, in the 80's, I started to get dissatisfied with my future possibilities. I realized that opportunities in Hungary during that time were very limited.

I loved animals and from a young age I had all kinds of pets, some I raised at a professional level. At one point I had over a hundred carrier pigeons and I was competing with them professionally. The pigeons were driven to far distances, often hundreds of kilometers away and they had to fly back home, competing with each other. I had a registered German Sheppard dog kennel, I raised and trained dogs and attended dog shows with them. I was fascinated by all this; it was a passion that I thought would become my career so I studied to be a veterinarian technician.

After graduation I could not find suitable employment in that field and I ended up working as a sales representative for a large manufacturing company. My colleagues were great, I learned a lot but I never lost that desire to accomplish more in life. It became clear that I would have to look outside of Hungary for the type of life and success I wanted.

One night I had a casual conversation with a friend of mine and we said – "what if we went to a Western European country where opportunities were limitless"?

That same night we decided to go to Austria which is the closest Western European country to Hungary. Many Hungarians chose that path to a better life in the past and we couldn't wait to follow their footsteps.

The next day I went to a government office to apply for a passport. My friend was a frequent traveler and already had all the required documents. He decided that while we wait for my passport he would go to Austria and research opportunities for us.

When he returned, his assessment was that Austria might not be the best choice for us. Things had changed there and someone recommended going to Spain instead. That was an unexpected change of plans, we did not have any information about Spain and never planned to travel that far.

Language was another challenge. I spoke some German at the time which could have been useful in Austria but none of us spoke any Spanish. We already decided to leave the country so there was no going back in our minds. Once I got my passport the following week we packed a small travel bag each, bought a one way ticket to Spain and off we went. The year was 1988 and we were only 22 years old, still living with our parents.

I will pause here for a moment. Note how easily we made such a big and life changing decision overnight. We had a burning desire to do something with our lives. When your dream is strong enough, no obstacle is big enough to stop you. I'd also like to point out the emotional aspect of this decision. Both of us were very close to our families and friends but could not tell anyone that we were leaving the country. We could not tell them because they would have considered this a crazy and dangerous idea. We barely passed our teenage years, did not speak the language and did not know anyone in Spain.

Instead we told everyone that we were going on a two week trip to a nearby lake. We thought this would buy us time so that no one looks for us right away.

I left a "goodbye letter" in a drawer for my parents, hidden among my documents. In it I explained that I loved them very much but I had to follow my dream to find a better future.

My brother was serving in the army at the time and wasn't home. We were – and still are - very close and I would have liked to say goodbye to him. Had he been home during that life changing moment, the outcome may have been different. I may have convinced him to come with us or he may have convinced me to stay. We'll never know.

Back to the story ...

Before we knew it, we were on the plane heading to Spain.

Madrid, Spain – picture by Gabor Balogh

Spain

Once we were in Madrid, it took us a few days to investigate what steps we needed to take to stay there legally. Once we knew that it was possible to stay we had mixed emotions, excitement and some sadness.

Excited for the opportunity to start a better life yet sad as we realized how far we were from everyone that cared about us.

I also had to face the most difficult task I've ever done - I had to call my parents and tell them the truth. With my heart pounding I called my father at his work (few people had phones in their homes back then) and explained briefly that I was in Spain. I told him that I was on a payphone and could not talk long but I left a letter behind explaining everything. I told him where the letter was and hung up.

It was heart breaking yet I did not understand the full weight of this phone call until years later when we met again. I learned that my parents were devastated and completely shaken to the core. They fell into depression and felt guilty as they blamed themselves for not being good parents. My father reflected on every disagreement we ever had and thought – "what if that was the reason why he left us".

Now as a father myself, many years later I get emotional when I think about this. Would I do it again if I could go back in time? – Probably not, perhaps I would have included them in the decision making. My father has passed away since and I cherish every memory I have of him. I have his voice recorded but haven't been able to listen to it since he passed, 16 years ago. It's just too painful. I will forever regret not spending more time with my parents and my only brother; it is the biggest price I ever had to pay.

Back to the story ...

It took us some time to properly settle down in Spain. At the beginning we slept at shelters with homeless people. Amazingly these places were very clean and well maintained. We even spent one night sleeping in a park and to this day I have the sleeping bag. At lunch time we lined up at churches where nuns were handing out free food to the homeless.

I guess we were temporarily homeless but we never saw it that way. In our minds we were on a mission and this was a small price to pay. At the time it seemed like an exciting adventure. We were dreamers and during the day, having lots of time on our hands, we visited expensive stores and luxury car dealerships. We pretended to be potential buyers at Ferrari and Porsche dealerships and we set in those cars to have a feel for them.

Eventually we had enough income to rent a room and got busy working in all kinds of jobs. Some of my jobs included; driving wealthy people around, delivering meat, construction, even housekeeping and babysitting. I wasn't afraid of work, I was focused on a better future.

A year later both of our mothers visited us which we financed with money we earned. That was a point in time when the healing process started for them. They could see that we were doing fine and started to realize that we did have more opportunities in a foreign land.

It was still hard as I did not return to Hungary for 6 years which meant I did not see anyone for that length of time – except for my mother of course. That was before Skype and video phones so I literally did not see my family and friends for 6 long years.

We learned Spanish faster and found better paying jobs sooner than other immigrants that had been in Spain longer. We were not smarter but our desire was stronger and our goals were clearer.

We had all kinds of jobs as I mentioned and were amazed at how much more money we made than back home. It was our first glance at capitalism and earning possibilities. (Since then Spain has gone through some challenging times and today our experience would be different).

After living in Spain for two years I moved to Canada and my friend got married and settled down in Spain. He and his wife live on the beautiful island of Palma de Mallorca. We don't see each-other often but our friendship remained special.

When I think of those two years in Spain it was probably the most exciting time of my life, despite of all the difficult circumstances. Our minds were filled with so many hopes and dreams that I blocked out everything else. That's what I remember vividly.

Canada – Gabor Balogh

Canada

I had an uncle in Toronto whom my family had not heard from for over 30 years. I arrived in Canada with the help of a family friend and together we located my uncle following an old address. He and his family received me with open arms and took me into their home.

My father and uncle – two of five brothers – had not seen or spoken to each other since they were teenagers. I called my father and put his brother on the phone. That was an amazing moment in time which I will never forget.

My uncle and his family put me in school to learn English and provided for me until I was able to find employment. I had my first job within six months of arrival and from that point on I paid my own bills and was self-reliant.

While I was still in school studying English (I was already fluent in Spanish) I worked in a Mexican restaurant. I was a fast learner and learned English very quickly. Within a year I spoke English fluently and got a job in a law firm through referral. I started as a messenger and worked my way up to a mid-management position in a few years.

About that time I also started a part time business which I ran for many years in my free time. That experience taught me valuable business and life lessons. To better myself I attended seminars, listened to audio recordings and read over a hundred books on business, investment and success. To further my education I went back to school and got a college degree with honours in Business Administration.

25 years passed since I left Hungary and started my journey to find a better future. I realized that one never really "arrives" as Success is a journey not a destination.

I learned another valuable lesson that goes like this - you could live in the best country in the world but if you don't have Financial Freedom you're not truly free.

Once I understood this I was on a new mission – to find ways to achieve Financial Freedom.

I will go into this in more detail in the following chapters.

What is success?

Picture by Gabor Balogh

Success means different things to different people. Relaxing under the palm trees on a tropical island is the symbol of success for many of us.

Based on our beliefs about success we could even have negative associations with it. For example if you believe that wealthy people take an advantage of poor people you might conclude that (financial) success is bad or unethical. Therefore at a subconscious level you will avoid becoming financially successful because you don't want to become a "bad" person.

Let's look at some of the different components of success. I'll use this very simple illustration to get us started.

At first glance who would you say is more successful?

1. John is the CEO of a large company and earns $500,000 per year.

2. Marie has a college degree and makes $60,000 per year.

Now let's take it further...

1. John's expenses per year are $510,000 – negative balance; no money left for investments or retirement.

2. Marie's expenses per year are $35,000 – positive balance; she has a growing investment portfolio.

3. Now let's take it even further...

1. John is so busy at work trying to finance his expensive lifestyle that he has no time for friends and family. In fact, his wife left him and took the kids.

2. Marie has a balanced lifestyle. She spends quality time with her family and attends her children's school activities. She even dedicates time to charity events and donates some of her income to worthwhile causes she believes in.

The outside world often judges someone's success based only on their position in life and their income level but as you can see using the example above the definition of success is complex.

We can conclude that John is successful in his earning ability but he's a failure in every other aspect of his life.

Marie on the other hand seems less successful at the beginning but definitely seems better positioned overall in the end.

In summary, the more areas of life you succeed in the closer you are to "true" success. The more "out of balance" your success is – meaning you succeed in one area at the expense of another area - the less likely your success will be long lasting. It's normal to be "out of balance" for a time period while you're focusing on a goal but your ultimate goal should be to achieve balanced success as soon as possible.

Long term success needs to be built on honesty and integrity. Success is like a house – the foundation needs to be strong all around – any weakness in the structure and it will collapse.

It takes discipline to reach success in every area of our lives. Discipline is a habit that you need to develop early on if you want to succeed. The more disciplined you are in one area the more likely you'll apply that discipline in other areas.

If you look closely, successful people develop different habits than unsuccessful people. Once they identify what daily steps they need to take to achieve a desired result – they keep to that daily routine, even if they don't feel like it.

Successful vs unsuccessful

Successful people think and act very differently than unsuccessful people. Let's look at some of the differences.

Successful people:

- Their outlook on life is very positive and they have high expectations
- They have clear goals and visualize the results they would like to achieve
- They focus on the solution
- They take responsibility
- They're eager to learn and get better
- They admire and respect other successful people – they want to learn from them
- Their priorities are in the right order
- They're very disciplined to do what needs to be done

Unsuccessful people:

- Their outlook on life tends to be negative and they have low expectations
- They don't set goals and tend to drift in life
- They focus on the problem and get paralyzed by it
- They blame others
- They think they already know everything
- They resent successful people and even accuse them of being lucky or unethical
- Their priorities are all mixed up

- They lack discipline and tend to do things when they feel like it

To be successful one has to develop the right thinking and daily habits that are the foundation of success. Once you have a handle on that you can apply it in every area of your life.

Remember: Start with small and easy steps. If you make it overwhelming to yourself your mind will reject it and will "give you" a good reason not to do it. It is very important to experience small successes along the way so that your confidence grows.

Don't be afraid to fail once in a while. Failures are an important part of your learning and growing. Learn from it and do it better next time. If someone never failed it means that they never tried hard enough to reach their full potential. Every successful person could tell you about countless failed attempts to achieve their goals until they finally succeeded.

Get outside of your "Comfort Zone". Comfort Zone is this box you feel comfortable in. Whenever you need to do something that is uncomfortable you are operating outside of your Comfort Zone. If you do it often enough it will get comfortable eventually. In other words you can get your Comfort Zone bigger by doing things you don't like doing. Successful people make it a habit to look for things they're afraid of doing and do it anyway.

"Everything you want in life – but you don't presently have – is outside of your Comfort Zone" (Source unknown).

Passion

Successful people are driven by passion. They might be passionate about their line of work or about the results they would like to achieve.

You love what you do - You love your occupation and it's also bringing you closer to your life goals. This would be the ideal combination and it produces the fastest result.

You love the results - You have a job or business you don't like but it's taking you closer to your dreams and goals you do feel passionate about. This will also work as long as you keep your eye on the target.

None of the above – You hate your job and you're not getting anywhere. You feel trapped and hopeless. Your first goal is to get out of this situation and find something you feel passionate about. Live is too short to spend it in this state of mind.

Emotional Intelligence

Someone can be very intelligent intellectually but still lack emotional intelligence. Emotional intelligence allows us to do what needs to be done despite of stress and negative emotions. It's not easy to stay calm when someone is negative, upset or even hostile towards you. You can learn, however to put aside all those negative feelings and deal with the core problem. In fact, that is the only real way to deal with it. If you reacted to a negative person with a negative attitude, it would be like trying to put out fire with fire.

When we have emotional intelligence we are in control of our emotions as opposed to being controlled by our emotions. We are able to make important decisions based on facts and not so much based on how we feel at the moment. Having said that, don't ignore your feelings necessarily as they can provide guidance. If you don't feel right about a situation it could be an indication that something is wrong and you picked up on it subconsciously. It could also indicate that you're making a decision "outside of your comfort zone", therefore it would be natural to feel uneasy and overwhelmed. If you review all the facts you'll be able to identify why you feel the way you feel, and ultimately your decision will be based on facts.

Comparing countries

Interestingly, poor countries are often very rich in natural resources and yet people struggle to survive and often go hungry.

The explanation for this is complex as you have many factors such as bad politics and corruption just to name a few.

However, my observation has been that, to a large degree, it also has to do with the mentality and mindset of the people living in that country. The more people you have in a given country that think and act like successful people the better the country does overall.

I think it's wonderful to help countries in need with money and food donations but until we educate them and show them how to think like successful people they will always rely on donations.

Influence from your environment

Success can be learned and the earlier in life we associate ourselves with successful people the better. Individuals who struggle or have a temporary setback, often shy away from successful people. They're insecure and feel jealous – they prefer to associate with others who are in similar situations. This is a mistake – you see, the only way to break the cycle is to learn from those who succeeded. Recently I was researching schools for my 5 year old daughter. There is a website that lists all the schools in the province, rating them using a point system. I found it very interesting that it even listed the average income of the parents.

Most people would agree that a school with a good rating is important, good and caring teachers are important – but few people would look at the average income of the other parents.

I believe it is just as important. I would look for a school that has the highest average parent income. Why? – Because I want my children to be surrounded by kids of successful people. Those kids learn different things at home, they have different conversations at the dinner table. I want my child to be influenced by those families.

This is not obvious, what is more obvious is when we analyze the opposite situation. When we look at housing projects where low income families are housed together in affordable buildings we can see that there is nobody to learn from about success. Sadly, these places often become negative influences for the children that grow up there.

No bad influence comes close to our prison systems. The expectation is that those who committed a crime will come out as better individuals after they had time to reflect on their past behavior. The reality is the opposite. They spend all this time with other, often more dangerous and more sophisticated criminals. Not exactly a positive learning environment to create honest and successful members of society.

Until a system is created that re-educates the minds and core values of those who ended up on the wrong side of the law, we are just adding to the problem. While I agree that certain crimes require tough punishments, I also believe that most people with minor offences could be positively influenced to change for the better.

Areas of Success

Areas of success could be broken down into many areas; I will just mention a few:

Relationships - Family, friends

It is important to give this area high priority as you are succeeding in life. It's easy to lose sight of it in today's busy world, thinking "I will spend more time with my kids or my aging parents when I have more time and money". In reality by that time it will be too late. The kids grow up very fast and you miss out on their childhood. Parents could be long gone by the time you're ready. The same applies to other important relationships in our lives. *Give quality time to the quality relationships in your life.*

At the same time spend your time "wisely". You may be spending time with the "wrong" people – people who hold you back in life or are bad influences for you. Don't be afraid to say "goodbye" to them. They might be well meaning relatives but their outlook on life is just too negative. You may not be able to eliminate these relationships but you can spend less time with them.

Remember: Your relationships in life have a great impact on your success. If you want to be more successful you need include successful people in your circle of influence.

Health

Intellectually we all acknowledge that we need to take care of our health. However most of us don't do enough to stay healthy. We "don't have time" to eat well or do enough exercise. One day when we are successful we'll have the time to get back on track. That time will never come because we never develop the habit – unless we make time today. Living a healthy lifestyle takes discipline. *If you live a healthy lifestyle, eat well, exercise and stay fit, it will give you more credibility in other areas of your life as well.* It will demonstrate that you have the discipline to do things well.

The good news is that you don't have to spend hours in the gym to stay fit. Exercising or going for a walk 15-30 minutes a day will keep you in a better physical shape.

Remember: You want to be in good health to enjoy the success you achieved in other areas of your life.

Spirituality

When we have a strong belief that we're not alone in the Universe and feel connected to a higher level of existence we seem to have more balance in our lives. We have a more positive frame of mind and seem to achieve more of our dreams and goals. We "attract" success into our lives. On the other hand when our outlook is negative and we're worried all the time we attract the very things we fear.

Some people feel spiritual through a religion of their choice and others through meditation and prayers.

Talking about spirituality is a relatively "safe" topic, however when we talk about religion in depth, it is a much more complex and difficult discussion.

The two should mean the same but there are differences.

While spirituality allows for an open mind and encourages learning and growing, religions often follow a strict interpretation and discourage their members from questioning what they perceive to be an "absolute truth".

"Organized religion emerged as a means of providing social and economic stability to large populations and it served to justify the central authority" (History of Religions- Wikipedia).

Though there are still some old ideas that hold us back from truly growing spiritually, I believe as we learn and mature our religions will be more spiritual and less political.

True spirituality is non-judgemental and we need to learn to respect other people's beliefs, allowing them to connect spiritually the way they find it fulfilling.

We need to keep an open mind and instead of convincing others of our ideals we need to understand their perspective. Seek to understand before you seek to be understood.

Keep in mind that we only use about 10% of our brain power therefore how we perceive and understand everything is still very limited. We must not come to the conclusion that we know everything and everyone else with a different opinion is wrong.

Many years from now, our great grandkids and their kids will most likely have a very different interpretation of spirituality, religion and what all that means.

There are great books on the "Law of Attraction" that explore this concept in detail. "The Secret" and the

"What the Bleep Do We Know!?" are good examples, both have movie and book versions.

Finance: This seems to be one of the last items on everyone's list to talk about. I think the reason is to be politically correct – so that we don't come across "materialistic". In reality this area is very important as it has a direct effect on almost everything in life.

Most people have conflicting believes about money, therefore they never have enough.

Let's look at this closely so that we can identify some of the negative associations.

- *"Money doesn't buy happiness"* - We all heard this overused phrase - by the way the lack of money doesn't make us happier either. Money does "buy" happiness indirectly, however. It buys you more time with people you care about. The number one reason why people get divorced is arguments about (the lack of) money. Money buys you the best medication and medical care for loved ones. Money donated to charities feeds hungry people. It also makes your life more comfortable and less stressful so that you can focus on the important things.

Happiness is internal and it comes from purposeful living. You have to feel happiness before you have money; otherwise you will be just as unhappy with money as you were without it.

- *"Money is the root of evil"* – I am still not sure if people actually believe this or they use it as an excuse to explain why they don't have any. Money is neutral – it will do good things in the hands of good people and bad things in the hands of bad people. In other words money brings out who you really are; it shows your true colours. We need more good people with money to do more good in the world.

- *"Wealthy people are greedy, I don't want to become one of them"* – There are greedy wealthy people and movies almost always portray them that way. But the reality is that many wealthy people are generous and spend time and lots of money on worthwhile causes. Once you get to a point where you don't have to worry about your own financial problems you have time to look around and see other people in need.

- *"Money is not the most important thing in life"* – true, not directly but money will greatly influence how you experience life. For one, when you have money you have time to think about what is important in life as opposed to worrying about bills.

Financial Freedom - Financial Independence

I find it interesting that different experts have different views on this.

Most financial professionals will advise you to gradually save up for retirement via various financial products so that when you are older you don't have to worry about money.

They look at your current income (as a limited pie) and make recommendations as to how to divide it, reduce expenses and use some of that money to save or invest for retirement. I think the problem for most people is that even if they save most of what they earn (living very economically) they would still not end up with enough coverage for retirement, especially if they live long. They never enjoyed today (trying to save every penny) and won't enjoy the golden years either. Let's say in the best case scenario they save up enough and have money during their retired years. They still have one problem: they spent their entire lives trying to save money and never truly enjoyed the younger years. If your only purpose in life is to save up for retirement then what's the point?

I do agree that investing for the future - especially for retirement - is important but it's only one part of the story. We have to look at a bigger picture and prepare ourselves to gain a better understanding.

The true definition of Financial Freedom is that you have enough money coming in now to cover your expenses regardless if you work or not. You're no longer worried about money; in fact you forget that money exists.

I have spoken to some very wealthy people who would definitely fall into the Financial Freedom category. They told me that when they lived paycheck to paycheck money was always on their mind. Once they achieved Financial Freedom they never had to think about money any more.

They would go to an expensive restaurant and never look at the bill as it was irrelevant. The price of the menu never entered their mind.

When you take financial worry out of your vocabulary – hopefully before you're too old to enjoy it – it changes everything.

Income types

Simplistically speaking there are two types of incomes:

Active Income

In this group people either have a job or a self-employed business. They have to be there to make the money and if something happened to their ability to work, their income would stop. Many people are educated and earn high incomes in this category therefore would consider themselves financially independent. They cover all their expenses and more, right? Yes, however they do depend on a job which could end along with their high incomes.

Passive Income

In this group people developed scenarios - through business, investments or any activity that pays royalties - where they receive ongoing income but no longer have to be there actively. In other words they did the work once and the income is ongoing, often passed on to generations. I believe that true Financial Freedom requires passive income.

Ironically many people in this category don't have the traditional educational background – what they have is street smarts.

Note: While I believe in traditional education, I also believe that it is no longer enough. For the most part, the school system teaches people how to be good employees in different professions but it doesn't teach people on how to handle their finances. To achieve higher levels of success one has to continually read educational books, attend seminars and associate with successful people.

I would recommend any book by Robert Kiyosaki who is very good at explaining this concept in easy to understand terms. In his book the "Cashflow Quadrant" he goes into this in great detail.

The phrase "go to school, get good education and find a good job" no longer guarantees success. Job security doesn't exist any more, even for highly educated people. I believe you should still get good education – if you can – and find a good job – if you can. BUT - remember that it may not be enough. You have to find ways to add passive income to your household income. That way you have more security as passive income could potentially cover your expenses in the future – if something happened to your job.

Compared to Employment (Unemployment) Insurance that may cover you for a limited time with a limited amount – passive income is yours to keep even if you don't lose your job.

You may decide to continue working even if you don't have to. I have heard of doctors who practised medicine for free in 3rd world countries as they no longer needed an income. Helping people was their passion and their passive income covered their expenses. OR you may decide to retire early.

I believe that Passive Income is the ultimate financial security, the True Financial Freedom.

Why are most people climbing the wrong financial ladder?

Let's take a look at where the financial advice is coming from in most cases.

Financial Planners: Interesting to note that many financial planners I met don't fully understand the world of passive income.

Most of them are employees themselves and not independently wealthy individuals. Their advice is mainly focused on "spend less than you earn (from your job) and save or invest some of your money so that you can retire comfortably".

Most earn commissions on the financial products they sell therefore their advice is not unbiased. Almost none of them will recommend that you increase your income or – more importantly - develop passive income so that you could replace your active income – while you're young enough to enjoy the results.

Part of the problem is that most people under the "Financial Planner" title are really insurance and financial products sales representatives. They're not really planning your financial future as the title suggests. In my mind a Financial Planner should have an unbiased opinion as they make recommendations based on what's best for you and not what's best for them.

If you want Financial Freedom you'll have to educate yourself on finance at least to the point where you can tell a good advice from a bad one.

Study wealthy people like Warren Buffett and others. Successful people often write books on how they achieved success, how they invest their money, etc. You'll find that their advice is very different from most Financial Planners which is a true eye opener.

A true Financial Planner only makes money when their recommendation produces positive results. Ideally they have personally achieved the financial results they're promising you and are willing to show you their own Financial Statement to prove it.

On the following pages I will list a few examples that would help you develop passive income.

Passive Income Types

Real Estate

I believe that everyone should own their own house or condominium. If you rent currently this would be the 1st goal to achieve.

Now, as usual, not all experts agree with this statement. They believe that house ownership is not for everyone. Some of their concerns are:

- If you lose your job you won't be able to make mortgage payments
- If you're close to retirement you don't want to carry a mortgage into your golden years
- In a bad housing market you could lose money
- You might end up with expensive repair costs

The list goes on and on.

The way I see it is very simple – if you pay rent you always lose money, actually you lose a 100% of the money you put in. When you own a property you can always sell it if times are bad. Even if the housing market is bad you will get money for your house. You won't have to give it away for free – which is what you're doing when you rent. You give away your money and you have nothing to show for it when you move out.

Look at it this way. If you and your family pay $1,500 rent for an apartment, in 10 years you would have paid $180,000 or in 20 years you would have paid $360,000 in rent. You could have a fully paid house with that amount and your housing expenses would get reduced by $ 1,500 per month.

Would you be closer to Financial Freedom with a fully paid house? Absolutely! You see, you can never even dream of being Financially Independent as long as you pay rent.

Once you have your own house you can take it to the next level – if using Real Estate to earn passive income appeals to you. You may decide to rent out a room to a student or your finished basement apartment to a family. They could help you pay your mortgage.

Once you gain experience with house ownership you may decide to buy additional rental properties and have the tenants pay for those mortgages. The money that is left after covering mortgage and expenses is your monthly passive income. (You also have a house that someone else is paying off for you).

This of course would become a true passive income opportunity once you hired others to manage your properties. As long as you are the one fixing toilets in the middle of the night for your tenants, one could argue that the income is not passive.

There are several good books on this topic written by Real Estate experts that could guide you through the process. Example for the Canadian market: "Real Estate Investing in Canada – How to Create Wealth with the Acre System" by Don R. Campbell. You can look up books and seminars in your country to properly prepare yourself.

Remember: Own at least one house – yours.

Stock Market

Short Term Approach - Buy and Sell

Most people try to buy low and sell high, hoping to make a fortune. This seems to be the most common way but the least predictable. No one can truly predict the ups and downs of the Stock Market therefore this approach – to some degree – is like playing the lottery. It also requires you to be involved very actively therefore it defeats the purpose if you're looking for passive income.

Long Term Approach - Buy and hold stocks that pay dividends

The big names in investing use a different approach which I personally like better. It is a more predictable approach with true passive income potential.

You can buy stocks that pay dividends on a quarterly basis. The idea is to hold on to these stocks long term so that you start developing regular income from these dividends. Ideally you would buy stocks from well established companies that have many years of history. As you buy more stocks and increase your portfolio over time you could start earning a decent passive income from these stocks.

When you use this approach you don't have to worry about the ups and downs of the Stock Market. You're not concerned about selling high – as you're holding on to your stocks that pay dividends.

Additionally you can participate in a "Dividend Reinvestment Program" where your dividend is automatically reinvested to buy more stocks. When the prices fall you're buying more stocks when the prices go up you're buying fewer stocks. Regardless, your dividend paying stock portfolio is growing. With this automated approach you can just sit back – once it is set up – and let your passive income grow.

If earning passive income from the Stock Market appeals to you there are excellent books on this topic. Example: "The Lazy Investor" by Derek Foster. He retired at the age of 34 using this approach.

Remember to always do your due diligence after reading a book by an expert. Some of the details could have changed by the time you read the book and the rules and regulation might be different in your country. Read such a book to get an overall picture then do your own research.

Network Marketing

This business model is often misunderstood and created mixed feelings in the world of business.

People actively involved in the business swear by it almost blindly. Some that did not succeed became negative and are completely against it. And of course many people barely know about it to have an opinion.

This created a lot of confusion about this business concept and even bad reputation.

I was involved in Network Marketing for over 10 years. I spent a lot of time with very successful people, learned a lot about business in general and gained a lot of understanding about this industry.

I would like to use this chapter to clarify some of the misconceptions that built up over the years so that you can decide whether this is for you.

Overall I believe that this could be a great financial vehicle to develop significant passive income if you have a very strong drive and motivation to do it.

History:

This business concept was born 80 years ago by a company that manufactured organic multi-vitamins. They called it "multilevel marketing" and set the foundation for this business model. The business concept went through several names and today it's called "Network Marketing" or "Direct Selling".

Basically the concept goes like this: You register with a company and get a business number. With this business number you are legally entitled to sell the company's products and/or services and keep the markup as your profit. This is no different than having your own franchise and run it as a self-employed business owner.

You can also recruit other people to join your "team" of business owners. They would be self-employed (just like you) and what they sell would be their profit. Additionally for developing a team of business owners the company pays you additional bonuses and a percentage of what your team sells. The more you sell and the more your team sells – the more income you make. Potentially this income could be unlimited and can grow to very large amounts. Over time you can have "passive income", once you developed an established team.

The question often asked is this: "Where does the income really come from In Network marketing?"

First of all you have a profit margin as if you had a traditional store. You buy a product for $3.00 and you sell it for $10.00. With today's technology like the computer and internet you don't actually buy the products in advance to resell them. You simply connect the customer to the manufacturer and keep your profit which is the difference between wholesale and retail.

The second level of income comes from building a team of people that also promote these products and services. The money most companies spend on advertising in this business concept is paid to you. By recruiting people and training them to sell and recruit others - you in fact become an "advertising agency".

This business model has been compared to pyramid schemes but it is really based on misconceptions.

 Pyramid schemes are illegal. Basically money is collected from a group of people and once a month the person at the top of this chain collects it all. The next month everyone remaining in the group puts money in but additionally recruits other people to do the same. They hope that in a few months they would be at the top collecting all the money. This goes on for a few months until someone at the bottom refuses to put more money in and the whole thing collapses.

This has been declared illegal many years ago but people still confuse it with Network Marketing occasionally. The reason – the recruiting aspect of Network Marketing resembles a pyramid scheme at first glance.

There are some fundamental differences, however. In Network Marketing money is exchanged for products and services and your position in the team does not guarantee income. If you work harder you can make more money than the person who brought you in.

While my opinion of Network Marketing is positive overall I also caution people to have realistic expectations.

Some of the mistakes that lead to failure in Network Marketing:

If you look at any Network Marketing company you'll see that most of the recruiting is done by people who are relatively new and have not succeeded yet. The successful ones are either retired or limit their time to training their groups. These relatively new and inexperienced Network Marketers often over-promise the potential in their presentations. They're too eager or often desperate to recruit more people.

The number one cause of bad reputation in Network Marketing is the fact that inexperienced people misrepresent the opportunity.

Many of these over-enthusiastic and inexperienced Network Marketers don't succeed in the end and often become the negative opponents of the industry later. Ironically they don't realize that they were part of the problem.

Training seminars and training materials (books and audio).

This is another "Catch 22" in this business and it has received some criticism over the years.

The training offered by the good companies is often very high quality, potentially life changing. It is very important to get continuing education and training in Network Marketing just like in any profession. Everyone who ever succeeded can testify to that.

BUT – many people "get lost" in this positive atmosphere where they no longer monitor their finances (money invested in the business – return on investment). Instead of running this as a business, some people live in this fantasy world where they spend everything they have and more on the business believing that – as long as they stay positive - one day as millionaires they can repay those credit cards and line of credits. Often these people leave the business with negative feelings and negative bank accounts.

It is very important to manage this just like any other business – constantly staying on top of your finances.

Network Marketing is not for everyone. The business presentations often make it seem easy but the reality is that it takes a lot of time, effort, discipline, work ethic, dedication and persistence.

It requires you to go "outside of your comfort zone" and you have to have a strong motivation to do it. If you're too comfortable you may not go "the extra mile" to make it in Network Marketing. But if you do – the success could be very sweet for you!

If you're researching Network Marketing as a possible option for you, consider the following.

Don't judge the business based only on the person presenting it to you. They could be inexperienced so you need to do additional research on the company and their marketing plan.

You have to believe in the product or service they sell otherwise it will be very difficult to promote it.

Watch out for companies that seem to charge too much sign up fee (registration and business ID number). Make sure they explain in detail what you're paying for; what's included in that fee; is there a money back guarantee.

This is important - the longer the money back guarantee is offered on the sign up fee the better. It means the company feels confident about their business model.

Today there are thousands of Network Marketing companies but only a handful of them are truly good opportunities. Check them out on the "Better Business Bureau" website to see if they are registered there. See what other certificates they have by other independent organizations or governments.

Make sure they have been around for at least 5 years, preferably 10 years or longer. The length of time they have been in business is a very good indicator.

Be aware of people who are actively involved with more than one Network Marketing company. You can't build a successful business that way. This type of business is built on rock solid loyalty. Do your due diligence, choose the company that you like and be a 100% loyal to that one company.

Network Marketing – Conclusion

Note: Network Marketing requires less capital investment to start than most opportunities that produce passive income. Another advantage is that you have a lot of guidance and training to keep you on track. What you learn via the continuing educational program is applicable in other businesses and in life. You also have a team working with you – you're not alone.

It will require, however a lot of "sweat equity" to build it up. Therefore this business will only produce passive income once you get to a well established level. It is possible to reach that level within 2-5 years but it may take longer based on the time and effort you put into it.

I believe that you go through so much personal growth and development in Network Marketing that no other business or industry compares to that. It's the ultimate success makeover on you as a person. Shy and introvert people turn into confident business leaders speaking in front of thousands.

If this industry picked you interest you can visit the Direct Selling Association's website to learn more about the different companies you can choose from.

Laundromat Business

If you had money to invest you may consider setting up a Laundromat. It requires minimum maintenance and the laundry machines do the work for you.

You have to do your due diligence to choose the right location and do a proper cost analysis.

Your initial investment would be to buy the laundry machines and other equipment. You could rent the location but the better option would be to purchase the building your laundry is in. The real estate appreciation could put money in your pocket if you need to sell the property down the road. In the meantime you could rent out other parts of the building while you're running your Laundromat. In other words you would multiply your passive income.

Some of the regular expenses include:

- Rent / mortgage on Laundromat facility
- Gas, electricity and water
- Property Tax and Insurance
- Business Tax and License
- Security Camera
- Trash collection and janitor services – if you outsource it
- Parts and repair costs

You could probably run this business working a few hours a week unless you hire someone to run it for you.

Someone else running it for you would turn this into a true Passive Income opportunity. However, it may be a good idea to run the business yourself first so that you fully understand it.

Note: With this approach you could reach a decent passive income relatively fast but you also require a significant capital investment to get it going therefore it's not for everybody.

Vending Machines

Similarly to the Laundromat business there is Passive Income potential with Vending Machines. These machines are your "employees" and do most of the work for you.

A Vending Machine business can include drinks, candy, gum, chocolate, food bars and salty snacks. You may decide to get bulk machines that dispense a handful of candy or nuts. The basic duties of a vending route include stocking the machines and collecting the money.

Once you establish your routine, the business is relatively easy to operate. Locate a wholesale food supplier to buy your products and determine how often to visit your locations to restock.

You can begin earning a steady income but your income will depend on the number of machines you have and on the quality of the locations.

One of the challenges is find the right locations. You want high traffic areas to make sure many people have access to your vending machines. You may decide to hire a professional locator to find good locations for you but make sure they're reputable. They can be researched on the Better Business Bureau's website.

In this business you need capital to start as you will need dozens of these machines to make a significant income. You will also have repair costs.

Your vending machines will have occasional breakdowns. If you have many machines, repairs can get expensive. You can save money by learning how to do your own repairs.

Note: A Vending Machine business can provide you with a decent income working just a few hours a week. This opportunity would of course become a true Passive Income earner for you if you hire someone to run it for you. That is a choice you can make later once you have built up your business.

Writing books

Writing books is another great and meaningful way to earn passive income. It's meaningful because you have created something that potentially adds value to another person's life.

Once you wrote a book, you can work with a publisher or publish it yourself online.

Each approach has advantages and disadvantages.

Publisher - The advantage of using a publisher is that your book is printed and viewable in the book store. Someone can walk by it and pick it up; it is more visible to your potential readers. You wrote the book and everything else is looked after by the publisher.

The challenge is to get a publisher work with you if you're not well known. You have to find someone who sees value in your material which can be a lengthy process. The publisher also takes a big cut of your profits.

Self-publishing – You can self-publish eBooks, and print on demand books on the internet.

This approach has many advantages. You have full control and once your book is written, it can be available online immediately. You have almost no expenses as you can ask friends and family to help you with editing and cover design. Alternatively you can hire professionals, like editors and graphic designers to package your book in a way that is more appealing to your audience.

It does take more effort on your part to get your book in front of readers. If you're not well known people won't automatically look for it online. You will have to find ways to promote it.

From the readers perspective eBooks are less expensive to buy than traditionally published books as some of the expenses are eliminated. From the author's perspective there is more profit potential with self-published books as you don't share the profit with the publisher.

Interestingly eBooks are now outselling traditionally published books.

There are several websites where you can sell your eBooks. Amazon's Kindle Direct Publishing has the biggest audience, therefore it might be a good place to start.

Createspace is a website where you can self-publish and offer print on demand books. This is a great way to reach out to those who still prefer paper books in their hands.

Both websites have cover design programs with templates that you can use for free.

You can create your own website and sell books directly to customers. It is possible to have a website for free using companies such as WordPress.com. You would need to set up your own payment method such as PayPal so that your customers can pay on your website directly. This option works well if you have high priced books that might not sell well on Amazon.

You can also use your own website to simply provide more information about yourself and your books and create a link to Amazon's sale page where the actual purchase would take place.

Once your book is available online, ask people you know to read it and write reviews on the webpage where the book is sold. Most people that don't know you won't be interested in a book that has no reviews posted, therefore you would need to have this done before advertising it.

Social media is a great place to let people know about your new book. You can use Facebook, LinkedIn, Twitter, etc.

There are many good books and internet articles that could help you with this process. One example would be a book called "Publishing E-Books for Dummies" by Ali Luke. It is very detailed and it gives you many good ideas.

What books would you write?

If you're a good story teller you may decide to write novels and fiction books.

If you have some great information to share based on your knowledge or experience, you can write a book on that topic. If you find that information helpful and useful yourself, chances are many people would benefit from it.

There is a great book on this called "The Millionaire Messenger" by Brendon Burchard. It talks about how you could become an expert on any topic that you're interested in.

Note: You can develop true passive income from writing books. You do the work once and you get paid ongoing – as long as your readers see value in it. You don't have to give up your full time occupation to write as you can do it in your spare time.

There are no guarantees that people will buy your books, especially when you're starting out as an unknown author.

As I write this book I have no way of knowing how it will be received by you, the reader.

I started out writing this as a booklet for myself to summarize the things I've learned and to remind me of the goals I still have to achieve. When I decided to make it into a book I included my story to give you a background on the author.

Conclusion

I personally believe in using a balanced approach to ensure that we're on the road to Financial Freedom and a Successful Life.

Yes, go to school and get good education – if you haven't already – but don't stop there. Read lots of books and attend seminars on a regular basis to continue your learning. To reach higher levels of success you have to continue developing yourself. Study successful people and learn to think like them.

Find a good job, but use some of your free time to work on your "Financial Freedom Plan". Just remember, don't use your employer's time to work on this. That would be unethical and you could not call yourself truly successful that way.

"How we do one thing, we do everything" (source unknown).

Make it your goal to do an excellent job wherever you go. If you work for a company, do the best you can and go the extra mile. You'll develop the habit of excellence and will apply that to your "Financial Freedom Plan" as well.

Use the traditional methods to invest and save for retirement but don't stop there. Look for ways to develop Passive Income so that one day you have more choices, financial security and hopefully Financial Freedom.

Working on this book has been a great experience for me.

You may be just starting out in life or starting over after some challenges. You could be very successful already but need an occasional reminder to reach higher levels of success.

I would like to thank you for your time and I hope you enjoyed reading my book as much as I enjoyed writing it.

Hopefully it added value to your life and made you think about your future.

Sincerely,

Gabor Balogh